About the a

Jackie Durnin has been interested i
years and has studied both Irish and
She recognised how many friends and family who were parents
for the first time experienced a lot of frustration when they did
not know what was wrong with their inconsolable child. Through
her research, she discovered the use of sign language in relation
to communicating with preverbal babies. As a result she
developed, Australian Baby Hands, a fun easy to follow guide for
parents, which incorporates the national language of the deaf
community of Australia, Auslan.

CW00402242

Published by:

Baby Hands Pty Ltd

Australian Baby Hands is an imprint and registered trademark of: Baby Hands Pty Ltd

More information about Australian Baby Hands and its products can be found at
www.australianbabyhands.com

Copyright © 2012 Baby Hands Pty Ltd

Design by Anneke Zilich, Medaltally Pty Ltd. annekez@medaltally.com
Photography & Signing Illustrations by Gary Capps
Produced in Singapore by TIEN WAH
Third Edition

ISBN 0-9757558-0-3

Dedication

For my Granny Catherine Durnin,
an inspiration and constant support in my life.
Thanks for always believing in me!

Contents:

Dictionary

V

What People Say...

"What a brilliant idea. I only wish Australian Baby Hands had been around when my children were tiny. Simple to understand and helpful on so many levels. More than that, an Australian first!"
LISA WILKINSON
Executive Editor of Madison Magazine, Editor at Large
Australian Women's Weekly, Host of Weekend Sunrise

"I have been in the child care industry for nine years. Australian Baby Hands is a very interesting read and a great concept. I think babies or even children should learn to sign and it should be a subject taught in Primary Schools."
KIRSTY GREENFIELD
Child Care Worker

"Australian Baby Hands is an incredibly interesting, easy-to-read guide to communicating with a baby before the baby develops its speaking skills. This book is invaluable reading for any parent or teacher."
KATRINA WALL
Primary School Teacher

"A clear and well researched book. I think it will be great for babies and childcare teachers."
ANNETTE BEX
Family Play Therapist

What Parents Say...

"A great read - you feel compelled to commence signing immediately and it is great fun for all family members."
SUSAN ROGERS
Mum to 18 month old Colm

"A very thought provoking insight into the world of sign language in relation to babies. A must read for any parent or parent to be. I will definitely endeavour to use signs with my baby."
DR. NATALIE DUMER
Mum to newborn Audrey

"A fun and positive way to assist with my baby's learning. I found this book to be an easy to read guide to introducing sign language into Sam's early development of communication skills."
KARINA LIDDELL
Mum to 6 month old Sam

"Two young children and a book that can save us (The Parents) from frustration. We found the philosophy behind the sign language fascinating. All of the signs are easy to follow. Thank you for opening our minds to 'sign fun' and allowing our youngest to start to communicate in ways well beyond other children of the same age."
PAUL & LIZ HUNTER
Parents of 4 year old Hayley and 9 month old Sarah

"After working with young children for years, I know the value of clear, effective two way communication. The very notion that the communication skills, and hence overall language skills, of my baby, can be developed using the "Australian Baby Hands" method excites me a great deal. Having us grow closer because of it will be an added bonus!"
SARAH JACKSON
Primary School Teacher and Mother to be

Foreword

The gift of communication between parents and their babies is one of life's true joys. For some, baby sign language offers a new and enriched opportunity to interact with their baby, learn more about them and their needs. For others, such as deaf parents, communicating through sign language is a way of passing on a much valued language and culture to their children.

While there are still many questions unanswered about all the benefits of baby sign language, we know that it can only enhance the relationship between babies and their parents.

The author, Jackie Durnin, has decided to use signs from an existing, formally authenticated sign language (Auslan), as they can lead all the family towards bilingualism, and the capacity to communicate with a significant group of people later on. The background information challenges us to consider the benefits of baby sign language, as identified in various research studies, but also wisely cautions us that all children and families are different and may see different results. She suggests some simple ways in which signs can be introduced in an enjoyable and fruitful way, during the parents' many daily interactions with their young baby, and with very little stress. In fact Jackie emphasises the need to have fun!

In a later section of the book, with attractive, clear and friendly photos, and with brief but very clear instructions, the reader learns how to make the first simple signs to use with their baby. We are happy to recommend this book to all parents who have an interest in early communication with their baby, and in the stimulation of their baby's mind in a happy, different way.

DEAF CHILDREN AUSTRALIA
www.deafchildrenaustralia.org.au

Acknowledgements

This book would not have become what it is today without the help, support, encouragement and advice from many people.

First and most importantly to my partner, Gary, who has been my best friend, my editor, my photographer, my rock of support and much much more. Without you, my book would not be what it is today!

I want to give a special thanks to Deaf Children Australia for their support and advice. I would especially like to acknowledge Lyn Wilson for all her help, support and suggestions.

To Anneke and Derek Zilich, my neighbours, my friends, my designer and my publicist. Thank you for transforming my work from a word document into a work of art. Your creativity, kindness, support, encouragement and friendship is something I will never forget. You guys rock!

Thanks to all the following people who have helped me on this journey: Jane-Monica Jones, Jane Holdsworth, Scott Fullerton, Fiona Scattergood, Jolie Compton, Romy Hodgson and Dorothy O'Brien. Also to all those who reviewed the book for me, thank you for your feedback and suggestions.

Finally, a huge thanks to all my friends, family and people I have met along the way who have helped me survive this whole process. Thank you all!

X

Introduction

$\mathcal{H}$ow many times have you looked at your inconsolable baby and thought; "Why is my baby crying?" You check if your baby needs changing, wants a drink, wants food or maybe wants their favourite toy, but nothing seems to work. If only they could tell you what they needed!

Some parents are lucky enough to find out what the problem is and solve it straight away. Others sit there helpless, confused and frustrated and hope that their baby will cry themselves to sleep. If only your baby could tell you what's wrong, what hurts, what they want or what they need, wouldn't it make your life a lot easier? Australian Baby Hands has been developed to help you overcome these frustrating times when you do not know what is wrong with your baby or what your baby wants. This book provides a fun way for you and your baby to communicate and help overcome or assist with these moments.

Did you know that some children of deaf parents have been known to begin communicating with their parents through sign language as early as eight months old whereas many children of hearing parents do not say their first word until they are around twelve months old? This shows us a gap of around four months and implies that babies are able to communicate a lot sooner than their oral motor skills would allow. Hearing babies, introduced to sign language, have been known to communicate as early as six months old. This book will help bridge this non-communicating gap between you and your baby and introduce you to the joys and benefits of Australian Sign Language (Auslan).

You can start to introduce your baby to this basic form of sign language at any age but at six months old your baby has the motor skills to sign back. Through baby sign language, they can let you know what they want, what they are thinking or what they are interested in. It provides you with an insight into your baby's view of the world!

Irrespective of whether you are a parent for the first time or for the tenth time, you will find that your most challenging role as a parent is understanding your baby's needs and wants in a timely manner so as to avoid these tear-filled frustrated moments.

Australian Baby Hands will highlight the research and studies surrounding the use of baby sign language. It will show how baby sign language can help towards stimulating your baby's brain development, increasing your baby's I.Q., improving memory and empowering your baby to communicate before they can speak. These are just some of the benefits that you could experience by introducing baby sign language into your home. Your individual baby's results may vary from the results given in the studies cited herein, due to many other factors influencing your baby's development. If you receive nothing more from this book than a stronger bond with your baby, I believe the adventure you are about to embark upon is well worth the journey. Have fun and enjoy getting to know your baby while learning the basics of a beautiful language, Auslan.

Chapter One

WHAT IS BABY SIGN LANGUAGE?

*B*aby sign language is the practice of using simple sign language or gestures to assist parents, family and child care workers to communicate with pre-verbal babies. By watching your baby, you will notice that it is a natural inclination for them to use their hands for visual communication. For example when your baby requests to be picked up, they will communicate this through a gesture of spreading their arms. Encouraging and developing natural movements such as these through simple sign language will improve the communication channels between you and your baby.

There are two predominant schools of thought concerning the teaching of baby sign language. One involves teaching your baby using symbolic gestures or made up signs. The other involves teaching the actual signed language used by the deaf community in that country, such as Auslan (Australian Sign Language).

The first approach was initially developed and used by Dr. Linda Acredolo of the University of California at Davis, and Dr. Susan Goodwyn of the California State University at Stanislaus. The scientists have conducted considerable research into baby sign language since the early 1980's and have co-authored a Baby

Signs book. They advised parents to create their own signs; signs that they believe their baby would respond to and be able to replicate. Their latest book now incorporates some ASL (American Sign Language) signs as well as symbolic gestures as its teaching tool.

Dr. Joseph Garcia and Dr. Marilyn Daniels are strong supporters of the second school of thought (both authors and researchers in the field). They highlight that using a signed language offers the advantages of standardisation and consistency and introduces your baby to a second language (bilingualism). Dr. Garcia wrote a thesis on baby sign language using ASL (American Sign Language) in 1987 and through his research concluded that hearing babies who are consistently exposed to sign language on a regular basis at six to seven months of age can begin expressive communication by their eighth or ninth month (1). Dr. Daniels has been involved in sign language research for over two decades. She advocates the use of sign language throughout a child's life and in particular in children's education. Her research highlights improvements in hearing children's English vocabulary, reading ability and spelling proficiency (2).

After weighing up the research, Australian Baby Hands has chosen to use Auslan as the basis for the baby sign language in this book. By using Auslan you are introducing an established Australian language. This way your baby may be exposed to an environment where all those involved in signing are reproducing the same signs consistently. This assists your baby with the learning process, opens them up to bilingualism and introduces the whole family to the basics of Australian Sign Language.

However, Sign Language is not a universal language. Just as there are different spoken languages around the world, there are over 140 different signed languages including Auslan, BSL (British Sign Language), ASL (American Sign Language), ISL (Irish Sign Language) and NZSL (New Zealand Sign Language). From these, Auslan, NZSL and BSL all have their origins in 19th Century BSL whereas ISL and ASL are more closely related to French Sign Language (3). These groups can initially be differentiated by the demonstration of their alphabet. Those with a BSL background use a two-handed alphabet whereas the other group use a one-handed system.

Auslan, although having its origins in BSL, has grown to be quite different over the years. As with different countries and different regions, there are different dialects and accents, this is also true with sign language. For this book Australian Baby Hands have incorporated the signs that are either the most common in all states of Australia or the sign that is the easiest for both baby and parent to replicate. These signs can be found in the illustrated dictionary in chapter eight.

Australian Baby Hands is not designed to enable you to have full conversations in sign language with the deaf community but to introduce you to some basic words in sign language for the purposes of communicating with your baby. This book also endeavours to show you the fun in learning this wonderful language and hopefully encourage you to pursue some further study.

3

Chapter Two

YOUR BABY AND THE STAGES OF DEVELOPMENT

For many years, Swiss biologist and psychologist Jean Piaget's (1896-1980) work was the most influential research concerning the stages of cognitive development in children. Cognitive development is a process whereby a child's understanding of the world changes as a result of age and experience (4). Piaget's theory suggested that children went through four separate stages of cognitive development in a fixed order and they could not perform certain tasks until they were psychologically mature enough to do so (5). Child development experts have begun to move away from these theories believing Piaget underestimated the cognitive capacity of children at these various stages (6). So what do the experts believe now? What is your baby capable of learning and holding onto in their mind?

Child development experts now believe that babies are capable of a lot more and at an earlier age than Piaget suggested. At the University of Minnesota, Associate Professor of Developmental Psychology Patricia Bauer conducted a study between January 1993 and June 1997 involving 360 babies aged 13, 16 and 20 months. The babies were shown how to perform six different tasks, one being to make a party hat decorated with various materials. The children were then encouraged to recreate the hat. Most of the children had no problem with this, as children love to imitate those around them. What is outstanding about this study is that one year later the children were called back to the university and asked to recreate the hat and these children could once again repeat the process of decorating the hat (7). This implies that babies' abilities are more advanced than Piaget believed.

So when does brain development begin and how can parents assist in this process? Well it all begins with your baby when they are in the womb. Billions of brain cells called neurons develop throughout the pregnancy. At birth your baby's brain weighs about 400g (more than one quarter of its adult size) and grows to around 1000g in the first year of their life. As time passes, especially within the first three years of your baby's life, inactive brain cells are eliminated. By the time your baby reaches adulthood; they will have half the number of brain cells than when they first started out life.

At birth, babies' senses (touch, hearing, taste and smell) are in perfect working order except for their vision, which only enables them to focus on items eight to twelve inches away. In experiments conducted shortly after birth, babies recognise their mother's voice and prefer her voice to other female voices. In the delivery room, babies recognise their father's voice and recognize specific sentences their fathers have spoken, especially if the babies have heard these sentences frequently while they were in the womb. After birth, babies show special regard for their native language, preferring it to a foreign language. Newborns also quickly learn to distinguish their mother's face and smell from all those around them (8).

Babies' brain growth, development and network building happens only once in a lifetime and as a parent you play a vital role in assisting and encouraging this process. To maximise your baby's continued brain development and learning, we need to encourage synapse formation. Synapses occur when there are electrical connections between the brain cells. Babies' environments and the stimulation they receive are the two major factors in encouraging these synapses to occur. A Psychiatric and Paediatrics Professor at George Washington University, Dr. Stanley Greenspan explains that your baby's brain development and growth is a combination of nature (your baby's genes) and nurture (your baby's surroundings, interactions, contact etc). In a study at the Baylor of Medicine, babies who were held and touched frequently and given the opportunity to play when young had brains 20% to 30% larger and had more synapses than children who had received less attention and care when they were babies [9].

Researchers have found that visual stimulation can produce developmental advantages including enhanced attentiveness, inquisitiveness and concentration [10]. It has been found that some of the best ways to stimulate your baby are in the following ways:

● Talk to your baby; your voice is a comforting recognisable sound to your baby.

● Encourage imitation; your baby learns through attempting to imitate those around them.

● Let your baby experience different surroundings by going for walks together, visiting friends and family etc.

● Interact with your baby through song.

● Provide a nurturing environment. Babies long for affection and love to be held.

- Play music for your baby; music has been found to stimulate the same neurons in the brain as the ones later used for mathematics

This combination of using visual stimulation, encouraging imitation and talking to your baby highlights to me that one of the best ways to assist with your baby's brain development while strengthening the bond with them is to introduce baby sign language into their everyday life. These very three things (visual stimulation, encouraging imitation and talking to your baby) are the basis of teaching baby sign language. Researchers have identified boosting your baby's brainpower as a one of the possible key benefits of baby sign language. I will discuss all the benefits, studies and research in greater detail in the following chapter.

Chapter 3

THE RESEARCH, FINDINGS AND BENEFITS OF BABY SIGN LANGUAGE

*W*hen people think of sign language, they think of a language used as a communication tool by deaf or hard of hearing people. This is not always the case. Since the early 19th century, sign language has also been used with hearing children to help improve language acquisition. Nowadays, sign language is also used with those who have Down Syndrome, Autism or other communication problems.

In the early 1980's, Dr. McKay Vernon and others discovered that all hearing children in his study who were born to deaf parents learnt to read before they began school thanks to their introduction to sign language and fingerspelling. He believed that this had great implications for the teaching of reading to all children. In 1985 a study conducted in the United States by Robert Wilson, Gerald Teague and Marianne Teague involved seven first grade students who were having difficulty learning to spell. Prior to the experiment, they could only spell 25% to 46% of their words correctly. In the experiment, the students were taught spelling using both fingerspelling and sign language to learn their words. Following this, the students could spell 56% to 90% of their words correctly. At the end of the study, the students were able to retain the spellings achieving 60% to 90% of the words spelled correctly (11).

A study conducted in Middlesborough, England, illustrated how sign language improved students' maths skills. For this study students were taught BSL and then taught the subject of maths entirely through sign. These students scored noticeably higher on their test scores compared to their peers who were taught in the traditional manner. The possible reason for this is that sign language, being such a visual language, fascinates children and causes increased curiosity, attentiveness and concentration; therefore causing greater mental retention and in this case, higher test scores (12).

These are only a sample of the early studies that illustrate the benefits of sign language and fingerspelling in the education of hearing children. Similar studies have been conducted in Belgium, Portugal, Sweden and the United States.

I would like to concentrate on the research that has drawn the most attention. Over the last two decades Dr. Susan Goodwyn and Dr. Linda Acredolo, two child development experts in California, conducted a landmark study in the field of baby sign language. In this study:

● Babies aged 11 months who used symbolic gestures had better language skills than their peers at two different time periods; a few months after the commencement of the study and again at the age of three.

● Sponsored by the National Institute of Health, after a period of eight years the researchers followed up on these children eight years later and found that the children who had used baby signs scored an average of 12 points higher than their peers in a standard I.Q. test. The researchers also took into consideration external aspects such as parents' income, education, and other factors that may have influenced the scores. These findings were presented at the International Conference of Infant Studies in Brighton, England (13).

Another prominent researcher in the field is Dr. Marilyn Daniels who is a Professor of Speech Communication at Pennsylvania State University. Dr. Daniels promotes the use of a national sign language in place of made up gestures. The main reason for stating this is that it furthers brain development and provides the advantage of a bilingual education. Dr. Daniels' research illustrates that using sign language from infancy through to the sixth grade results in improved literacy. The children she has worked with demonstrate better recognition of letters and sounds, better spelling, and larger English-language vocabularies than children who were not taught sign language (14).

From all the studies conducted in this field the benefits of introducing your baby to sign language are vast.
Baby sign language;

1. CAN EMPOWER YOUR BABY TO COMMUNICATE WITH THOSE AROUND THEM BEFORE THEY ARE ABLE TO SPEAK.
This means that your baby may be able to communicate what they want when they want it. It may also enable them to initiate a conversation about topics that interest them. Furthermore it bridges the gap between no language and spoken language.

2. CAN REDUCE FRUSTRATION FOR BOTH YOU AND YOUR BABY.
Sign language may allow your baby to tell you what they want, what's wrong or what hurts. Therefore your baby

may experience less frustration, tantrums and crying. If your baby is able to communicate their basic needs to you, it means you do not have to try and interpret their cries. Sign language can help reduce those tear-filled frustrated moments.

3. CAN ENRICH THE PARENT-CHILD RELATIONSHIP.
By introducing baby sign language into your home, you are enhancing the bond with your baby. The nature of Baby sign communication leads you and your baby towards responding to each other in turn and this is a really valuable skill. Signing involves daily interactions with your baby that will eventually lead to a two-way conversation.

4. CAN PROVIDE AN INSIGHT INTO YOUR BABY'S MIND AND WHO THEY REALLY ARE.
Baby sign language allows your baby to initiate a conversation with you about what they are interested in. It allows you to see what they are thinking, what they are interested in and what the world looks like from their view. All this before your baby can talk!

5. CAN PROVIDE A STRONG FOUNDATION FOR EARLY LITERACY AND LANGUAGE DEVELOPMENT.
Signing babies can have a better recognition of letters and sounds, better spelling and increased vocabulary skills. In one of Dr. Acredolo and Dr. Goodwyn's studies (which involved 43 children), the children demonstrated that by age two, they had a vocabulary of about 50 more real words than children not exposed to sign language. In another study by the scientists, three-year-old signing children had developed the language skills and vocabulary comparable to a four-year-old (15).

6. CAN STIMULATE INTELLECTUAL DEVELOPMENT AND IMPROVE MEMORY.
Children are fascinated with sign language and often pay greater attention to what is being taught when it is involved. It has also been shown that when children learn a word in conjunction with the sign, they are more likely to remember the meaning of the word (12).

7. CAN ACCELERATE THE SPEECH PROCESS.
Dr. Acredolo and Dr. Goodwyn's research has shown that children who use sign language may acquire spoken language faster than non-signing children (15).

8. CAN ENHANCE A BABY'S CONFIDENCE, SELF-ESTEEM AND SELF-EXPRESSION.
Due to a baby's ability to communicate their needs, wants and interests through signing, a baby may become more confident.

9. BABY SIGN LANGUAGE CAN STIMULATE BRAIN DEVELOPMENT AND POTENTIALLY INCREASE YOUR BABY'S I.Q.
Teaching sign language can stimulate your baby's brain development. Dr. Acredolo and Dr. Goodwyn's research has illustrated that signing babies achieve higher scores on future I.Q. tests (up to 12 I.Q. points higher) than children who learn to speak in the traditional manner (13). Dr. Daniels also agrees that signing can stimulate brain development as when learning sign language you use both the right and left hemisphere of the brain compared to learning a spoken language, which only uses the brain's left hemisphere. This use of both hemispheres results in the brain building more synapses (14).

10. CHILDREN WHO KEEP UP SIGN LANGUAGE ARE EFFECTIVELY BILINGUAL. By introducing your baby to signs from Australian Baby Hands, you are introducing your baby to a second language. Brain research suggests that language skills are acquired best in the first years of a baby's life. Also, by introducing Auslan to your baby and continuing to use this wonderful language after they can speak, you are giving your child the gift to communicate with the Australian deaf and hard of hearing community in sign language.

From the above studies, there is an extensive list of possible benefits involved in the teaching of sign language to your baby.

One piece of research conducted by Johnston, Durieux-Smith & Bloom in October 2003 assessed a number of baby signing programs on the market (ASL based material) and their supporting research concerning the benefits involved [16]. From this study, benefits such as increased vocabulary, advantages in language acquisition and a higher I.Q. were called into question. The researchers concluded that the use of sign language with the children involved in these studies could not be deemed the sole reason for the benefits they experienced. Other factors such as the parent skill level, the children's I.Q. prior to using sign language and the training in sign language received by parents were possible factors in the results achieved. Also the amount of quality time parents involved in baby sign language spent with their children, compared to parents who did not use a baby-signing program may have contributed to the results.

Australian Baby Hands is committed to trying to assess all the research involved in baby sign language and evaluate both sides of the story.

Keeping this in mind, Australian Baby Hands has been written as a fun way to learn to communicate with your baby while learning the basics of a wonderful language. Any input from you into your baby's early development years can only be of benefit. Whether or not you and your baby experience some or all of the above benefits should be just an added bonus to the process of learning baby sign language.

Chapter Four

INTRODUCING BABY SIGN LANGUAGE INTO YOUR HOME

Most parents have probably introduced some form of sign language into their baby's life without even realising it. For example waving goodbye and hello or perhaps nodding your head for 'yes' are a form of signed language. Introducing sign language into your home is a simple step and this chapter sets out a few guidelines to help you on your way.

1. STAY SIMPLE AND START SLOWLY.

    When you introduce signing to your baby, gradually introduce the signs one at a time. It is recommended to begin with approximately five words and once your baby has begun to respond to those words, you can introduce more. Sign language can be a slow process depending on the age of your baby when you begin. A six-month-old who is introduced to signing may begin signing back to you anywhere from one month to six months later; it simply depends on each individual child.

2. BE PATIENT.

    Every parent has the ability to teach his or her baby sign language. A major downfall for some parents is their lack of patience. Signing is not something that will happen overnight, it is a relatively slow process depending on each individual baby. Do not be discouraged. Your baby is learning from you and will, when the time is right, let you know that they understand through signing. This learning process introduces invaluable interaction with your baby. Do not give up whatever you do. Be patient and reap the rewards of sign language.

3. BE CONSISTENT.
Once you have decided on your initial five words, be consistent in using them with your baby. For example, if you are using the sign 'milk' with your baby and introduce this sign when you are feeding your baby, be sure to continue to use it every time you feed your baby. If you only use this sign now and again, your baby is less likely to understand that this sign represents 'milk'. They may think it is simply a game you are playing with them. The key here is to incorporate sign into your everyday life. Each time you use the word 'milk', develop an automatic reaction to sign and say the word out loud. Repetition is the key to success.

4. SIGN ON YOUR BABY'S LEVEL.
When you interact with your baby, it is important that you are on their level. Keep your facial expressions and signs within their field of vision. This ensures that your baby is seeing the correct way to sign the word. By signing at an angle to your baby, your baby's view of your sign may be totally different to the one that you are attempting to create.

5. USE BABY SIGN LANGUAGE IN CONTEXT.
When teaching baby sign language, it is importar
the word to the current situation or feeling of the mom...
There is no point in attempting to introduce your baby to a
sign when that particular sign represents something that
has happened in the past. For example, if you go for a walk
with your baby and see a dog on your walk, there is no
point on the following day, in signing the word 'dog' and
saying "Remember the dog we saw yesterday in the park."
Australian Baby Hands recommends finding as many situ-
ations as possible, in the present time, to use the sign that
you are attempting to teach. For instance, use the sign for
'dog' as you read a story about a dog, watch a dog on televi-
sion or point at your family pet.

6. ALWAYS USE THE SIGN AND THE SPOKEN WORD TOGETHER.
Ensure that each time you sign a word; you accompany it
with the spoken word. This enables your child to make the
connection between the two more quickly.

7. USE MOTIVATING SIGNS.
It is important when choosing your initial words that you
use a combination of 'practical' words and 'motivating'
words.

'Practical' words highlight words that will make you and
your baby's life easier once sign language is in use in your
home. These words are more general words and include
words such as eat, drink, change, pain, sleep etc.

It is important to balance these words with words that are
motivating or interesting to your baby. 'Motivating' words
may include words such as teddy bear, ball, play etc. These

are specific things that your baby may have shown an interest in.

8. TEACH FAMILY MEMBERS AND CAREGIVERS.
    It is important to introduce the signs you are using with your baby to people who are in contact with your baby on a regular basis. This will ensure consistency. The more your baby sees the signs, the sooner your baby will begin to sign back. Childcare facilities are slowly beginning to introduce signing to their day care so be sure to continually update them on what signs you are using with your baby.

9. USE AN APPROPRIATE FACIAL EXPRESSION WITH A SIGN.
    This is especially important when teaching feelings or sensations to your child. Sign language is a very visual language and members of the deaf community use their face as part of the signing process. When expressing a feeling, allow your face to vividly illustrate the feeling. A feeling of happiness can be illustrated with a big smiling face while signing and saying the word. A feeling of fear can be illustrated with frowning eyebrows or a startled look. Some words do not require or do not have an obvious facial expression. To animate your face is initially a little strange for beginners to sign language. To practise, stand in front of a mirror and see if you would know from your facial expression what word you are trying to sign. Remember you are better to over-express than under-express your signs with your face.

10. ENCOURAGE YOUR BABY'S ATTEMPTS.
    When your baby begins to sign, they probably will not initially get the sign 100% correct. It is important though to praise them for their efforts and repeat the sign correctly

back to them. When the child is showing you that they need something, give it to them, even if the sign is only approximately correct. They will begin to realise that it works!

11. HAVE FUN.
Sign language is a beautiful visual language and not one to get stressed about. If you are stressed when signing, your baby will pick up on this. Signing should be fun for you and your baby. It should not feel like a chore but be a part of your everyday life. Relax, have fun and enjoy the benefits that this wonderful language can bring to you and your baby.

Chapter Five

SIGNING WITH YOUR BABY

*T*he next step to signing with your baby is to familiarise yourself with a few basic everyday signs. The most common and favourable introductory signs for parents to use are Milk, More, Eat, Drink, Mum and Dad. As mentioned in the previous chapter, introduce a 'practical' and 'motivating' word to encourage your baby to engage in sign language with you.

It is important for you to look natural when signing. If you look frustrated, confused or stressed, your baby will pick up on this. Your baby will not want to learn something that will cause them frustration, something that is clearly not fun. When you have completed reading this book, practise the introductory signs until you know them without looking them up in the book. Then begin to incorporate these signs in your daily life while talking, singing or going for a walk.

It is important to remember that there is no clock ticking; you are under no time pressure. Take your time and enjoy learning this new language while teaching your baby how to communicate using sign language.

So when is the right time to introduce your baby to a sign?

Dr. Joseph Garcia outlines in his book "Sign With Your Baby" three different 'Gazing Moments', which are the most opportune times to show your baby a new sign. These 'Gazing Moments' are classified as follows:

• EXPRESSIVE GAZES
These moments occur when your baby has a want, need, feeling or question. This gaze is used often at mealtimes when your baby has finished their meal but is not full. You will notice that your baby makes eye contact with you as if to say, "I want more". This is a perfect opportunity to introduce the sign for 'more' and to give them more food or drink.

• CHANCE MUTUAL GAZES
These moments occur when both you and your baby make eye contact at exactly the same moment for no particular reason. When you catch your baby's eye like this, it is a perfect moment to introduce or reinforce a sign. For new signs simply pick up something close by which is of interest to your baby, perhaps a teddy bear, and sign that.

• POINTED GAZES
These occur when you and your baby look at an object and then at each other. These provide an opportunity for you to introduce this object to your baby through sign language. This is their way to express what interests them in the world around them.

You can use these 'Gazing Moments' as well in your daily routine with your baby to introduce and highlight signs. The initial baby signs that you introduce will generally surround the routines of eating, drinking, bathing, sleeping or changing. As these events occur frequently every day, they are a great way to establish sign language in your home. Let's now discuss how to integrate sign language into these daily routines naturally.

SIGNING NATURALLY

Lets start with a typical day in the life of a parent with a young baby. Use your daily routines to assist you with learning this new language.

CHANGING A NAPPY
Imagine that your baby is upset and crying as they have a wet nappy and need to be changed. It is important to make eye contact with your baby and be on your baby's level and within their field of vision before you begin signing (refer back to the tips in chapter four to help you get started). As you begin to change their nappy, sign the word 'change' as you say the word 'change'. Repeat this a few times until you have completed changing their nappy. Some parents move their baby's hands to replicate the sign. This can help your baby understand what you are trying to achieve.

MEALTIMES
There are a number of words in the dictionary at the back of this book that will be useful during mealtimes. These words include eat, drink, finished, food, milk, more, water, hot and cold.

At each mealtime, you should sign the word 'eat'. Always remember to follow the sign with saying the word out loud and repeat this action to help your baby associate the spoken word and the action. When it is nearly time to eat again, you could quizzically look at your baby and sign, 'eat', as if to say "Are you hungry?"

At a later stage, you can introduce more words to enhance this mealtime experience. For example when your baby has eaten their food, you can introduce the sign 'finished' while showing them the empty bowl. Again consistency and repetition is the key. Each time your baby finishes something, whether it be food, drink or reading a book, you can sign 'finished'. Another word which can be very beneficial during meals is the sign for 'more'. To introduce this sign, start by serving your baby a smaller portion than usual. Once your baby has finished eating the contents of their bowl, sign and say with a quizzical look 'more?' Encourage your child to sign 'Yes' or 'No' and follow through with the request. You can then add the remaining food to their bowl and sign 'more'. When your baby has finished the second serving, it is a good time to sign the word 'finished', indicating it is all gone.

Each time you give your baby a drink, again make eye contact with your baby while signing and saying the word 'drink'. At a later stage you can introduce the different types of drink to your baby, for example 'water' and 'milk'. Again when introducing additional signs, ensure they are a combination of signs your baby is inter-ested in (motivational signs) and practical signs. It is crucial to introduce to your baby the signs for foods and drinks that they love. By doing this you will be introducing signs to motivate your baby to learn more sign language. Also by encouraging your baby to replicate the signs, and rewarding them for their attempts, your baby will soon realise that to get what they want, they can com-municate with you through sign.

The signs for 'hot' and 'cold' can be introduced in relation to food, drink or bath time. Allowing your baby to touch a little cold water while in the bath can be an opportunity to introduce the sign 'cold'. Alternatively this sign can also be demonstrated by playing with an ice cube with your baby. As for the word hot, by simply showing your baby a piping hot dinner or a hot drink of yours and signing the word 'hot' are a couple of examples of how to teach these signs to your baby. The key to illustrating these signs is in the facial expressions accompanying the signs. Remember the more animated your face, the easier it is for your baby to understand what you are trying to tell them and the more fun they can have with you while learning.

BATH TIME

This time allows you to introduce words such as 'bath', 'cold' and 'water'. Every time you give your baby a bath, sign the word 'bath'. When it is time to introduce further signs, you can use signs such as 'ball' and 'fish'. Through singing, talking and playing games in the bath, you can make this learning experience fun.

PAIN

An important word to teach your baby is the sign for 'pain'. All too often parents have watched their baby's face screw up in cries of discomfort or pain but due to a lack of communication; they can only offer a shoulder to cry on. Australian Baby Hands offers you something more.

The next time your baby injures their self in some way, use this as an opportunity to introduce them to the sign for 'pain'. While comforting them, express both through your facial expression and through the sign, the word 'pain'. Again reinforcement and repetition is the key to your baby understanding what it is you are attempting to communicate. You can illustrate the sign 'pain' anytime anyone hurts himself or herself; if you stub your toe; if someone falls over. Use it at every painful opportunity and soon your baby will be communicating to you through sign language when they are in pain.

It is a good idea to use the sign 'where' and a pointing finger, in conjunction with the sign for 'pain'. This way when your baby is in pain, you can ask your baby 'where?' and encourage them to point to the part of their body that hurts. Again this can be encouraged initially by demonstrating the sign 'pain' with your baby's hands and then pointing to the painful part of the body. This technique of demonstrating with your baby's hands would be better accomplished when it is someone else in pain and not your baby!

Finally, it is important that you do not "drill" your baby with signs. In the early days of introducing signs into you and your baby's life, there will be a learning curve. You will not always remember to do the sign when engaging in the action; you may even demonstrate the sign incorrectly. Don't worry! This is not a test. Baby sign language is about interacting with your baby, enjoying yourself and learning a wonderful language. So remember whatever you do, have fun.

Chapter Six

A WHOLE NEW WORLD

*I*n the final chapter there is a dictionary of over 50 sign words to help you get started on the road to baby sign. This language will open up your eyes to a whole new world, a world through your baby's eyes. Baby sign language will allow you to gain an insight into your baby's mind, what interests them and their view of the world.

The previous chapter offered you ideas on how to introduce the basic signs through your everyday routines. An alternative way to do this is through song. Three different studies in the U.S. proved there are benefits to help enhance vocabulary by combining sign and song. One such study divided eighty children into four different groups to improve their vocabulary. The groups were taught through the following means:

- SIGN AND SONG
- SIGN AND SPOKEN WORD
- SONG ONLY
- SPOKEN WORD

The outcome was that the children who used a combination of sign and song had the biggest increase in vocabulary (17).

Over the next few pages I have included a number of songs to highlight different signs to your baby. Try them out and remember have fun!

This first song can be used to introduce your baby to various different animal signs. The following signs can be incorporated into the song in place of the bold words:

Cat	**Meow Meow**
Dog	**Woof Woof**
Kangaroo	**Boing Boing**
Koala	**Zzz Zzz(sleeping sound)**
Mosquito	**Bzzz Bzzz**

Old MacDonald

Old MacDonald had a farm, eieio

*And on his farm he had a **CAT**, eieio*

*With a **meow meow** here and a **meow meow** there*

*Here a **meow**, there a **meow**, everywhere a **meow meow***

Old MacDonald had a farm, eieio

The next song is a good song to introduce both actions and emotions to your baby. The following signs can be incorporated into the song in place of the bold words:

Happy
Cold
Hot

If You're Happy And You Know It

If you're **happy** and you know it, go like this:
(sign the word **happy**)
If you're **happy** and you know it, go like this:
(sign the word **happy**)
If you're **happy** and you know it, and you really want to show it,
If you're **happy** and you know it, go like this:
(sign the word **happy**)

The following song can incorporate many words from the dictionary in chapter eight such as:

Ball	**Blanket**	**Book**
Drink	**Milk**	**Teddy**
Telephone		

I've Got The Whole World

I've got my **teddy**-bear in my hands
I've got my **teddy**-bear in my hands
I've got my **teddy**-bear in my hands
I've got my **teddy**-bear in my hands

Chapter Seven

THE ROAD TO COMMUNICATION

*C*ongratulations, you are now well on your way to opening the doors of communication between you and your baby. Through a combination of daily routines, rhymes and songs, sign language will begin to become a part of you and your baby's everyday life and end those moments of frustration.

Again the key is to be consistent, repetitive and never give up. Enjoy discovering the world through your baby's eyes and the wonders of a beautiful language, Auslan.

I hope this book has provided you with an insight into the powers of communicating through sign language with your baby and ultimately that you have lots of FUN using Australian Baby Hands in your home!

Chapter Eight

DICTIONARY OF SIGNS

*O*ver the following pages you will find an introductory dictionary of signs to start you on the road to communicating with your baby. Each page of the dictionary contains a photograph of the sign. Accompanying each photograph are symbols indicating the movement of the sign and an explanation on how to do the sign.

Symbol Descriptions:

⟶ Movement in the direction indicated by the arrow. The length of the arrow may give an indication to the distance of the movement. The shape of these arrows may be curved

⟷▶ The first movement is towards the double arrow head then back to the single arrow head and then again towards the double head again. For example using this arrow the movement would be right left right. These arrows may also be curved.

This part of the hand or body should be kept still while making the sign.

 Wiggle the fingers two or three times.

 Move the hand along the path of the arrow. Do not change orientation or handshape

 A horizontal or vertical black line through an arrow means that the movement of the hand must remain on the plain throughout

 A line drawn across the tip of an arrow indicates a stop to the movement. Sometimes there may be contact with another part of the body

 Two parallel lines at the end of an arrow signify an abrupt stop to the movement of the hand. Sometimes there may be contact with another part of the body

 The double line arrow indicates the stress and speed of the movement

 Change the orientation of the hand as the hand follows the direction of the arrow. This will mean that the palm of the hand will face in a different way at the end of the movement.

31

aunt

*With closed fists and both thumbs protruding,
move hands in and out ensuring
the thumbs touch.*

32

baby

*Rest one hand on top of the other and
sway the arms from side to side
as if rocking a baby.*

ball

*With open cupped hands facing each other,
move hands down slightly as
though catching a ball.*

34

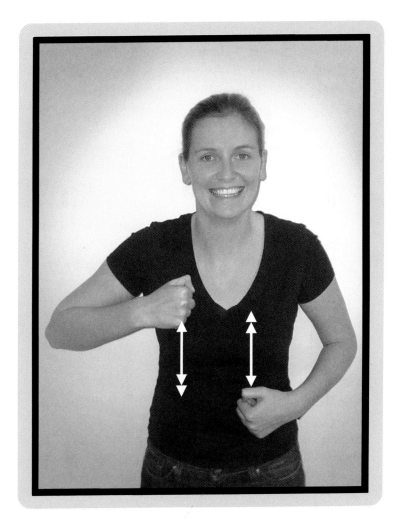

*With clenched fists, move the hands in opposite
directions up and down the chest
as if washing yourself.*

beach

*With open palms, move hands up and over
as if signifying a rolling wave.*

36

Place palm of hand on face and move head slightly down as though resting your head on a pillow.

37

bird

*Place right hand in front of mouth and use your index finger
and thumb to represent a beak. Allow the thumb and index
finger to touch and move apart to demonstrate
the beak opening and closing.*

blanket

*With closed fists, move your hands from waist level up and in
to chest level as though you were pulling up a blanket.*

book

With flat open palms and both hands touching,
allow your palms to touch and move apart
as if to open and close a book.

brother

With closed fists and hands touching,
rub hands in an up and down motion.

41

car

With closed fists, both hands are at positions of '10' and '4'
around the chest area. Move the hands in opposite directions
to each other as though you were steering a car.

42

*With both hands flat and palms down, gently brush the back
of your left hand with your right hand as
though you were stroking a cat.*

change

With index fingers pointing and hands at waist level, move the hands up and over allowing them to cross each other.

44

With clenched fists at chest level, hunch your shoulders and move your fists in and out in opposite directions as though you were shaking with the cold.

dad

*With closed fist, extend index fingers. Place right hand above
left hand and tap the right index finger off
the left index finger below.*

*With an open palm, gently pat your thigh
as though calling your dog.*

drink

With your hand in a 'C' shape, move your hand from chest level to your mouth as if signifying taking a drink.

With all fingers touching your thumb, move hand towards the
mouth as though you are putting food in your mouth.

finished

With closed fist and thumb extended (a thumbs up position),
rotate hand in a left to right movement.

*With a flat open palm at waist level, wiggle your fingers in
unison while moving your hand out from your waist,
like a fish swimming.*

goodbye

With open palm at chest level facing outwards, move hand in a right to left movement to signify waving.

grandfather

(Grand) With hooked index and middle fingers placed either side of nose, move hand in a downward direction.
(Father) With closed fist, extend index fingers.
Place right hand above left hand and tap the right index finger off the left index finger below.

53

grandmother

(Grand) With hooked index and middle fingers placed either side of nose, move hand in a downward direction.
(Mother) With flat open right hand,
tap fingers on the side of your head.

happy

With open palms, keep left hand still while circling the right hand towards the left hand and clapping the hands.

hello

*With open palm at chest level facing outwards,
move hand out to the right.*

56

*With right hand finger tips touching an open left hand palm,
without moving the position of the right hand, move both
hands simultaneously away from the body.*

hot

With open palm, place hand at right hand side of the mouth and move hand down and out in a semi-circular movement.

house

*With flat open palms facing each other and the tips of your
fingers touching, separate the hands and move them
out and down as though drawing the
outline of a house with your hands.*

hungry

With fingers bent and palms facing mid section, place fingers
on mid section and turn hands downwards
ending with palms facing away from you
(like emptying your stomach).

I love you

(I) With a closed fist point your index finger at your chest.
(Love) With flat open palms facing you,
cross arms and place them on your chest.
(You) With a closed fist point your index finger
away from you towards your baby.

kangaroo

With slightly downward curving palms, move hands simultaneously in an upward semi circular motion creating a bouncing action.

62

*With your hand in a claw like position,
palm facing you, place hand
over nose and mouth.*

milk

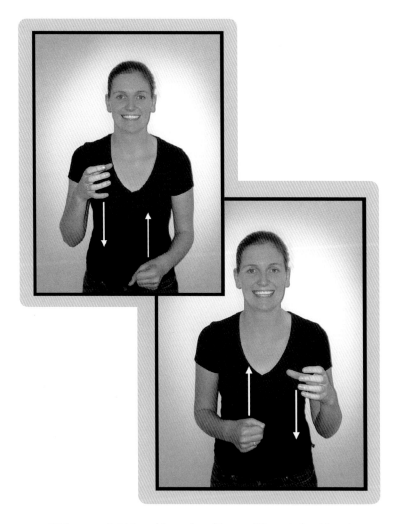

*With your right hand in a claw-like position at chest level,
squeeze the hand down into a closed fist to waist level.
At the same time, with left hand start with a closed
fist at waist level and do the opposite.*

64

With your hand in a claw-like
position touching your chest,
move your hand outwards.

mosquito

With your right hand in a 'C' shape, have your index finger and thumb touching. Make a circular motion with your hand as if to signify a mosquito flying around.

66

*With flat open right hand,
tap fingers on the side
of your head.*

music

With fingers and thumb touching, extend index finger and move your hands as though conducting an orchestra.

no! _{No!}

With bent wrist and closed fist, move hand sternly to the right.

69

pain

*With open palm facing inwards, shake hand
in an up and down motion.*

70

*With open palms face up, move hands in a circular
outward motion keeping at the same level.*

please

With flat palm, touch chin with fingertips and move hand up and out.

Pinch nose with index finger and thumb.

rain

With hands above shoulder level, move downwards
simultaneously like a downpour of rain.

74

scared

With your hand in a claw-like position at chest level, move hand in and out while touching the chest.

75

sister

With closed fist and hooked index finger, tap nose twice.

76

*With both flat open palms facing downwards,
lower hands downwards from chest level.*

sorry

With open palm and fingers slightly bent,
wave hand across mouth.

stop

*With flat open palm facing away from you,
move hand forward stopping abruptly.*

sun

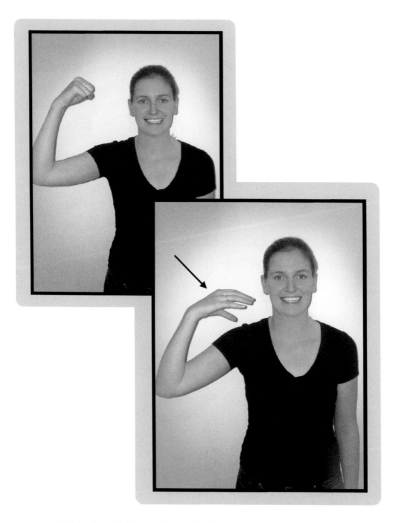

*With closed fist at the side of your head, move hand
downwards while opening your fist.*

80

teddy

With closed fist and index finger extended, move fingers in a semi-circular motion as though tracing a teddy bear's ears.

telephone

*With thumb and little finger extended,
simulate using the telephone.*

82

television

With closed fist and index finger extended, touch index finger off the side of open palmed left hand. Then make a 'V' shape with right hand and place it on left hand palm.

thank you

*With flat palm, touch chin with fingertips
and move hand up and out.*

With fingers slightly bent at chest level,
move hand outwards away from body.

uncle

With closed fists and both little fingers protruding, move the hands in and out making sure the little fingers touch.

With flat open left palm facing upwards, make a 'V' shape with your right hand and move hand along palm with a brushing motion.

87

water

With closed fist and hooked index finger, brush index finger in a downward direction on your right cheek.

With both flat open palms facing upwards,
move hands slightly from side to side.

yes

*With closed fist, move hand down and up by bending
at the wrist, as though nodding your head.*

90

FOOTNOTES

1. "Sign With Your Baby", Dr. Joseph Garcia 1999-2005 www.sign2me.com
2. "Dancing With Words: Signing For Hearing Children's Literacy", Dr. Marilyn Daniels 2001
3. "Sign Languages...", Interview on Lingua Franca 8/5/1999 www.abc.net.au/rn/arts/ling/stories/s25222.htm
4. "Jean Piaget's Theory of Cognitive Development", Rebecca Kodat 2002 Pagewise
5. ATHERTON J S (2003) Learning and Teaching: Piaget's developmental psychology [On-line] UK:
   Available: www.dmu.ac.uk/~jamesa/learning/piaget.htm
6. "Educating Psychology: Constructing Learning", McInerney & McInerney 1994
7. "Baby Brainpower", Gail Rosenblum
   www.sesameworkshop.org/sesamebeginnings/library/articlephp?contentId=860
8. "Babies are Conscious", David Chamberlain Phd. www.eheart.com/cesarean/babies.html
9. "Fertile Minds", J. Madeleine Nash, Time February 3, 1997 VOL. 149 NO. 5
   www.childcareaware.org/en/dailyparent/0397
10. "Building Baby's Intelligence: Why Infant Stimulation is Important"
    www.envisagedesign.com/ohbaby/smart.html
11. "The use of signing and fingerspelling to improve spelling performance with hearing children."
    Wilson, Robert M. / Teague, Gerald V. / Teague, Marianne G.: In: Reading Psychology: An International
    Quarterly 5: 3-4 (1984)-pp. 267-273
12. "Sign Language: The Best Second Language?" Steve Kokette
    Indy's Child: Central Indiana's Parenting Resource October 01 2000
13. "The Long Term Impact of Symbolic Gesturing During Infancy on I.Q. at Age 8", Linda P. Acredolo &
    Susan W Goodwyn, July 18, 2000 : Brighton, UK
14. "Sign , Baby, Sign!", Kristin Snoddon, WFD News, Magazine of the World Federation of the Deaf May 2000,
    Vol. 13 No. 1
15. "Impact of Symbolic Gesturing on Early Language Development", Susan W Goodwyn & Linda P Acredolo (2000),
    Journal of Nonverbal Behaviour, 24, 81-103
16. "Baby Talk!", Johnston, Durieux-Smith & Bloom, Canadian Language & Literacy Research Network October 2003
17. "The Effect of Singing Paired with Signing on Receptive Vocabulary Skills of Elementary ESL Students", Heather
    A Schunk, Journal of Music Therapy: Vol. 36, No. 2, pp. 110–124

REFERENCES

Acredolo, L., Goodwyn, S. and Brown, C.
"Impact of Symbolic Gesturing on Early Language Development", (2000) Journal of Nonverbal Behaviour, 24, 81-103.

Acredolo, L. and Goodwyn, S.
"The Longterm Impact of Symbolic Gesturing During Infancy on IQ at Age 8",
Paper presented at the International Conference on Infant Studies (July 18, 2000: Brighton, UK)

Acredolo, L., Goodwyn, S. and Adams, D.
"Baby Signs: How to Talk to Your Baby Before Your Baby Can Talk", 2002

Acredolo, L., Goodwyn, S. and Moore, B.
"Symbolic Gesturing and Joint Attention: Partners in Facilitating Verbal Development", April 2001

Berck, J. "Before Baby Talk, Signs and Signals",
New York Times January 6, 2004

Bernal, B. & Wilson, L., Deaf Children Australia, "Dictionary of Auslan", 2004

Brady, D. "Look Who's Talking - with Their Hands", Businessweekonline August 14, 2000

Collier, L. "Talk to the Hand: Babies' Sign Language 'tells' parents what they want",
Chicago Tribune February 27, 2000

Davidson, H. "Sign Language: Enhancing Language Development in Infants and Toddlers",
(1999) Drury College Summer

Elliott, J. "How baby signing aids communication", BBC News October 6, 2002

Felzer, L. "MBR Reading Program:
How Signing Helps Hearing Children Learn to Read - Research Summary", August 2000

Garcia, J. "Sign With Your Baby: How to Communicate With Infants Before They Can Speak", 1999-2005

Jaworski, M. "Signs of Intelligent Life", Family Circle, October 3, 2000

Johnston J., Durieux-Smith A., & Bloom K.,
"Baby Talk!", Canadian Language & Literary Research Network October 2003

Kokette, S. "Sign Language: The Second Best Language", Indy's Child:
Central Indiana's Parenting Resource October 01 2000

Kokette, S. "Hearing Students, Sign Language, and Music: A Valuable Combination", 1995

Lipari, J. "Raising Baby: What You Need To Know", July 2000

Morris, E. "Babies Can Use Sign Language", Insider Reports, November 02, 2000

Nash, M. "Fertile Minds", February 3, 1997 Vol. 149 No. 5

Rosenblum, G. "Baby Brainpower",
www.sesameworkshop.org/sesamebeginnings/library/article.php?contentId=860

Savory, E. "Baby Signing", CBC News Online March 10 2004

Royal Institute for Deaf & Blind Children, "Auslan Signbank", 2004

Snoddon, K. "Sign, Baby, Sign!", WFD News, Magazine of the World Federation of the Deaf May 2000, Vol. 13 No. 1

Stuever, S. "Better than Baby Talk: Sign Language for Toddlers", Mothering July-August 2004

Wilson, Robert M. / Teague, Gerald V. / Teague, Marianne G. "The use of signing and fingerspelling to improve
spelling performance with hearing children", In: Reading Psychology: An International Quarterly 5:3-4 (1984)-pp.
267-273

92